# STEPS

*to*

# GREATNESS

## DR. D. K. OLUKOYA

**Steps to Greatness**

© 2014 DR. D. K. OLUKOYA

ISBN: 978-978-920-052-8

Published July, 2014

Published by:
**The Battle Cry Christian Ministries**
322, Herbert Macaulay Street, Sabo, Yaba
P. O. Box 12272, Ikeja, Lagos.
www.battlecrystore.com
email: info@battlecrystore.com
        customercare@battlecrystore.com
        sales@battlecrystore.com
Phone: 0803-304-4239, 0816-122-9775

*I salute my wonderful wife, Pastor Shade, for her invaluable support in the ministry.*

*I appreciate her unquantifiable support in the book ministry as the cover designer, art editor and art adviser.*

All the Scriptures are from the King James Version

# CONTENTS

# ▶ CHAPTER 1

# The
# PREPARATION

*"Then the word of the LORD came unto me, saying, Before I formed thee in the belly I knew thee; and before thou camest forth out of the womb I sanctified thee, and I ordained thee a prophet unto the nations. Then said I, Ah, Lord GOD! behold, I cannot speak: for I am a child. But the LORD said unto me, Say not, I am a child: for thou shalt go to all that I shall send thee, and whatsoever I command thee thou shalt speak. Be not afraid of their faces: for I am with thee to deliver thee, saith the LORD. Then the LORD put forth his hand, and touched my mouth. And the LORD said unto me, Behold, I have put my words in thy mouth. See, I have this day set thee over the nations and over the kingdoms, to root out, and to pull*

> *down, and to destroy, and to throw down, to build, and to plant."* Jeremiah 1:4-10

The above Bible passage makes it clear, that God knew you before you were born. He knew you, before and after your mother conceived you. People will call you great names after you have become great, but God made you great, before you were great. What matters, is what God has made you to be from the beginning.

Every man and woman of destiny, who is assigned to be great must pass through the school of God's preparation. Many people desire to function powerfully. They desire to do well, but they are not really ready to pay the price of being ready for the task. Only few people are willing to pay the price of being ready for the task ahead of them. Men and women of destiny in the Bible were prepared by God before they could function well.

# THE PERIOD

The period of preparation varies from person to person. Each man and woman of the Bible were trained differently. For each man and woman of destiny, God has prepared a ready made school for each person. He has prepared the school depending on the kind of work He wants you to do, or what He wants you to fulfill. The intensity of divine dealing with your life will now depend on the programme He has for your life.

To prepare, is to make ready. To prepare is to make something suitable. To prepare is to train for a specific task. To prepare is to rehearse ahead of time. Preparation precedes manifestation. When Noah was building the ark, there was no rain, but he prepared. It took God forty years, to prepare Moses for the task He had for him. It took God twenty-five years to prepare the heart of Abraham for Isaac.

It took Joseph thirteen years of preparation, before he became the prime minister. It took Joshua forty years, before he began to lead Israel. It took Samuel thirty years, before he began to manifest. It took David sixteen years of preparation before he became the king. It took our Lord Jesus Christ thirty years of preparation before He began his ministry. It took Paul fourteen years before he could start anything.

## YEARS OF PREPARATION

Anybody who has produced anything worthwhile must have put in long years of preparation before achieving the goal. God's dealing takes time. He has to fortify you before He commits great thing into your hands. It is therefore a crime for a man who is not ready when his time comes.

It is your private preparation that will lead to public manifestation. The more successful you are in the school of divine preparation, the more impact you are going to make. When you are a failure in the school of preparation, you are likely to be a failure in the field.

Many people are grappling with the rehearsal now. A lot of people are faced with all kinds of problems. What you are calling a problem is just a rehearsal and not a destination. Before David could manifest he rehearsed in the field with his sheep. He fought with the lions and bears. He fought in the wilderness before he could face Goliath. David was already a small boy of warfare by the time he got to the war front and defeated Goliath. He did not wake up one day to fight Goliath. David was in the school of divine preparation in the wilderness.

## DIFFERENT TENOR

God prepared Moses with rearing cattle. For him to understand how to live with a large group of people, he started with cattle. So he understood the different kinds of sheep he was rearing. Moses had forty years of rehearsal with the back side of the desert. Peter was prepared with his fishing profession. He had imbibed the ruggedness and patience of a fisherman. The hard work of a fisherman was his second nature. When Jesus said, "Peter I will make you a fisher of men", he was telling him something he knew.

Many people are not ready to kill their Goliath because they are not rehearsing. They are failing in the school of rehearsal. Herein lies a great problem. In the divine school of preparation, until you have passed a subject, you will not receive a honourary pass. If in the school of divine rehearsal, God is teaching you how to padlock your mouth and keep it shut, but you have not learnt any lesson, you will keep getting into trouble until you learn those relevant lessons. In your school of divine preparation, God might want to cut off from you all the spirit and manifestations of anger, if you do not pass that school, your anger will keep getting you into a mess. A lot of people are grappling with the rehearsal now, and they think it is a problem. They ought to pick up the lessons the Lord wants them to learn.

## HOW TO SUCCEED

Do you want to pass your rehearsals? Then;

1.  **You have to discover the purpose of God for your life.** You must know, why He has sent you.

2.  **Develop a regular and consistent life of prayers.**

3.  You must read, and study harder.
4.  **You must learn from every mistake, and experience of life**. You must learn from your mistake. Only a fool does not learn from his mistake. They say, a sign of insanity is, to continue to do the same thing and you want    different results. It is abnormal to increase your speed when you have missed the road.
5.  **Do not excuse the defects in your character, deal with it**. Deal with your weaknesses and defects of character. This means that you must work on yourself everyday. You must not be satisfied with the average. You must move with those who will increase you and move you into a higher realm.

You must live with those who can lift you up. But if God has promised to take you to the highest mountain and you are satisfied with the valley, you will remain at the valley. God will never give you more than you can adequately handle. How you perform at the rehearsal will determine your level of progress.

## PRAYER POINTS

1.  Anything, that is planted in my life, to demote my destiny you are a liar, die, in the name of Jesus.

2.  Power of failure, loose your hold upon my life, in the name of Jesus.

3.  I will finish this year stronger, than I started, in the name of Jesus.

# CHAPTER 2

# EIGHT
## STEPS TO
# GREATNESS

To attain greatness in life you have to provide answers to certain crucial questions. The attempt to provide answers to these questions will make you a man or a woman of purpose. Purpose is the forerunner of success. Purpose can only emerge when you provide answers to soul searching questions. With this exercise you will never be the same again. You simply have done practical searching of your heart. The reply will help you to come up with purpose for living.

It is not difficult to know that only very few people think. While thinking may look quite natural, it is a very hard occupation, and sometimes, a very dangerous assignment. Only very few people do serious thinking, and even fewer people engage in serious meditation. It is a fact that a lot of people do not really settle down to think about the world in which we find ourselves and about life in general. That is why the Bible says, "O that they were wise, they would consider their end" Even many do not think about their personal life, and the devil ensures that people waste time, thinking about un-important things. This is why you have to ask yourself these eight questions:

1. What can you see?
2. Where am I now?
3. Who am I?
4. Why am I here?
5. From where am I coming?
1. Would I be made whole?
2. What happens when I die?
3. When the Son of Man comes shall he find faith in me?

If as a Christian you had never really thought of these questions or meditated on them, then you need serious prayers, because they are indeed serious eternal issues. Let us consider them one after the other:

## 1. WHAT CAN YOU SEE?

Let us go to the book of Jeremiah. The Lord asked Jeremiah another interesting question.

"Then the Lord said unto me, Out of the north an evil shall break forth upon all the inhabitants of the land. Then the word of the Lord came unto me, saying, Before I formed thee in the belly I knew thee; and before thou camest forth out of the womb I sanctified thee, and I ordained thee a prophet unto the nations. Then said I, Ah, Lord God! behold, I cannot speak: for I am a child. But the Lord said unto me, Say not, I am a child: for thou shalt go to all that I shall send thee, and whatsoever I command thee thou shalt speak. Be not afraid of their faces: for I am with thee to deliver thee, saith the Lord. Then the Lord put forth his hand, and touched my mouth.

*And the Lord said unto me, Behold, I have put my words in thy mouth. See, I have this day set thee over the nations and over the kingdoms, to root out, and to pull down, and to destroy, and to throw down, to build, and to plant. Moreover the word of the Lord came unto me, saying, Jeremiah, what seest thou? And I said, I see a rod of an almond tree. Then said the Lord unto me, Thou hast well seen: for I will hasten my word to perform it. And the word of the Lord came unto me the second time, saying, What seest thou? And I said, I see a seething pot; and the face thereof is toward the north. Then the Lord said unto me, Out of the north an evil shall break forth upon all the inhabitants of the land".*

Jeremiah 1:4 -14

So, I ask you the same question; what do you see? Was it that the Lord did not know what Jeremiah saw? Why was he asking that question? The Lord may be showing you the vision of your life and you may not see it. Your spiritual vision may have what you call spiritual cataract, which can prevent you from seeing what the Lord wants you to see. If you have made up your mind on what you want to do before you come to the Lord, and say, O Lord show me the way, you can be rest assured that you will not see anything, for you have already made up your mind on what to do before coming to the Lord.

Beloved, perhaps you are without a vision or plan for your Christian life, you really need to pray. The voice of the Lord is asking you, what do you see? God never calls a meeting for entertainment. At the Mountain of Fire and Miracles Ministries, for example, there is no room for satanic entertainment. There are lots of entertainment churches all around, for those wanting to be entertained. God has a serious purpose for bringing people to fellowship at MFM. God has

His distinctive purpose and He has no useless exercise. Even if the whole world is aimless and purposeless, God has a purpose for everything he does. God believes in man so much that He invested heavily in you, by allowing His son to die, and He expects returns from you. If I may ask you this question: Do you know for sure what is happening to you? What stage are you in the history of your life?

Have you seen the personal vision God has for you? Do you know your purpose in life? If you do not know the vision of God for your life, then, you will not be able to plan. God does not experiment for He knows what He is doing. The earlier you find out what He wants you to do, and you begin to do it, the better. God is called the Alpha and the Omega because before He starts a thing, He has completed it.

God never starts a thing without finishing it. God determined that Jesus was to be born, and that he would die to redeem man. All these were clear in His mind before he started to look for Mary who would deliver the child. Why did God conceive you? Do not be one of those people getting confused, or prospering in the wrong times. The fact that what you are doing is prospering does not mean it is right. Please close your eyes and pray seriously to the Lord this way: "Open my eyes to see your purpose for my life, in the name of Jesus."

Now there are two ways to recognise those people who do not have visions for their lives. They will prophesy and disobey the prophecy. They will be the ones to say, my servant, my servant, I want to use you mightily. But it is the same person that gave the prophecy that will be committing sin. People always move from one business to the other without making headway, they do not really know what God wants them to do. They choose their spouses through physical observations. They receive direct messages from the Lord and then throw them aside. They want to lead others, but they do not want to be led. Any small failure experienced will get them discouraged. These are the people without visions.

For somebody who knows what he has seen, all the discouragement and failures on the way are nothing but fertilizers. Those without vision are the ones who see men looking like trees. They criticise others concerning sins which they themselves commit. They do not know whether they are hearing from God or the devil. There are many of them in the churches agitating for church posts. Some find it hard to serve the Lord unless they are in the leadership position.

Many of us often dream, but how many of us know what we are dreaming about? Have you got to that level when you will be having a dream and right there in the dream, you will be asking the Lord what the dream was all about? Not that you will wake up confused and then start praying for the meaning of the dream for three months without an answer. No, you have to do better than that.

## 2. WHERE AM I NOW?

*" And the Lord God called unto Adam, and said unto him, Where art thou? And he*

> *said, I heard thy voice in the garden, and I was afraid, because I was naked; and I hid myself."* Genesis 3:9-10

In contemporary English the question becomes, where are you? What an interesting question! Was it that God did not know where Adam was? The question was asked because Adam was no longer in the right place, he had left where God wanted him to be. Adam was found in the wrong place, God changed His original intention for him. He threw him out of the garden and put an angel with the sword of fire at the gate, so that the man would not find his way back there.

Know this beloved, that when you depart from the path of God for your life, a forty days journey will take forty years. It is a pity that many people have never really found out God's plan for their lives, but have abandoned the plans after listening to people of the world. I do hope you know that money, education, and material possessions, are not signs that you are enjoying God's blessings. The sign can only be seen in you when you are at the centre of God's will.

Are you at the centre of God's will for your life? Or are you like David who stayed at home while others were fighting, or Peter who stayed in the wrong place. No wonder then that Peter at a point in time started to follow God from afar. Are you in the wrong place in your carrier, business, or spiritual life? When you are in the wrong place, you cannot receive God's blessings. All that you can get are crumbs here and there. You will not be in correct fellowship with the Lord and this will make you an easy target for the devil. When God asks, where are you? The meaning is, where is your spiritual location in God? What do you weigh in His balance?

Nebuchadnezzar was a very great king, and there had never been a kingdom so great in splendour and might and glory like the Kingdom of Babylon that Nebuchadnezzar was ruling. But God dealt with him when he got too proud. God sent him into the bush and humbled him completely. He ate leaves like animals. Whatever you are doing, whether good or bad, God has His weighing balance. So if God were to put you on His scale at this moment, where you are will determine your balance on the scale.

A lot of people's weight are equal to zero. Ask yourself, where am I in the spiritual scale of the Almighty? If you love yourself say, "I refuse to be used as a bad example in the name of Jesus". When you are not where you should be, you can become an easy target for the enemy.

What is your spiritual temperature? Perhaps the Lord has searched for you amongst divine dreamers, visioners, prophets, etc, and your name was not in any of these places. Then suddenly, the devil shouts saying, "God, I have his name in my evil books! I have her name in my terrible records". The voice of the Lord is ringing out to you today loud and clear saying, "Where are you?

A lot of spiritually lame people come to church. Their gifts of vision have disappeared. They were on fire before, but now they have become cold. We have spiritually deaf and dumb people too in large numbers in many churches today. They do not hear from the Lord neither do they see any vision. They do not comprehend anything. It is not surprising at all that such people invest even in wrong places in the physical world. Your answer to this question is very important: Where are you? Belteshazzar eventually knew where he was. God told him that he had finished the arithmetic of His kingdom, weighted it, and found him wanting.

Please close your eyes and talk to the Lord about yourself this way: "Set my life on fire for you and bury all my lukewarmness, in the name of Jesus. Looking inward, are you still being harassed by the spirit of fear. If the kind of things that used to put your heart on the race is still doing so now, it shows that you have not grown at all. Perhaps your faith is still as rudimentary as when you just believed.

Perhaps your knowledge of God is so hazy that you have never used the name of Jesus to defeat any power of the enemy in your life. Perhaps you have been a believer for one year or two and you cannot differentiate between the voice of the Holy Spirit, your voice, or the devil's. The solution is to seek for help and not to console yourself by saying that you are better than someone else.

## 3.   WHO AM I?

That is the question of identity. You may be putting yourself into trouble if you are ignorant of your identity. If for example you are walking along the street, and a policeman asks you to identify yourself, your identity card, which reveals who you are, must be produced. Failure to produce an authentic identity card in such a situation causes trouble. The Bible tells us that man was made in the image of God. He was a free, rational person and quite different from animals. The Bible says, each person is a spirit, living in a body and having a soul. God ·made the man and the woman, but because they both sinned, they were both cursed.

We are all made in the image of God, but, unfortunately, that image has been defaced and spoilt, and man is lost. He has no hope in this world, or even the next.

Man is a lost soul, walking about in the wilderness. And it is only by giving his life to Christ that he can find his way out. The question of identity is so important that apostles of old were asked questions which pertained to their identities. In John1:22, John was queried by the Jews who were in doubt about his identity and therefore asked him

> *"Then said they unto him, Who art thou? that we may give an answer to them that sent us. What sayest thou of thyself?"*John 1:22

John the Baptist, then, answered:

> *"He said, I am the voice of one crying in the wilderness, Make straight the way of the Lord, as said the prophet Esaias."* John 1:23

God has a general purpose for all of us, but you must know who you are. If you do not know who you are, then you are opening your door to problems. The lesson on identity is an important one. Jacob learnt that lesson; he knew that by his identity he was not in the place of blessing. If you have read the Bible, you will discover how he used foul means to get his brother's blessing. He got it by claiming his brothers' identity.

Let this be clear in your spirit, that one of Satan's most effective devices is to get people to doubt their identities. He did it to Jesus, that if He was the Son of God, He should command stones to become bread. He did not stop at that. Again, he told Jesus that if He was the Son of God, He should cast Himself down. And when Jesus was on the cross, Satan came again to tempt him. He told Jesus that if He was truly the Son of God, He should come down from the cross. It is therefore possible for the devil to challenge you by saying, that if you are truly a child of God you should not be suffering.

It is wise for you to know the answer to the important question which says: who are you? That is why as a believer you should not confess negatively e.g. "I am not worthy. I am worn out. I am unfit," etc. That was your old identity tag. But once you have given your life to Jesus, and if by the grace of God you are living the kind of life God wants you to live, you should not call yourself strange names again. If you still do, it means you do not know who you are.

The prodigal son was rotten and bad. At a stage, he came to himself and remembered who he was; he remembered that he was a son and not a slave. Therefore you too must remember who you are. When Jesus was in the world He did not hide His identity. He identified Himself as the Light, and the Bread of life. The Bible tells us what our identity is. It says that we are the branches, new creatures and not refurbished ones. The Bible says we are God's workmanship, we are more than conquerors, and our lives are hid in Christ. All these point to our collective identity, and you must know them.

Do not be like Peter, who was released from jail, and did not know because he was surprised. The day you know that you belong to God, your Creator, that day you will begin a victorious life. At this juncture, I would like you to pray this way, "O Lord show me who I am in the spirit, and open my understanding, in the name of Jesus." It was possible for Elijah to do exploits for the Lord because he realised his position in Jesus, he knew his identity early enough. Who are you then in the spiritual scale of the Almighty God? What can you use to identify yourself in the spirit? Please pray again that the garment of ignorance should be roasted, in the name of Jesus.

## 4.    WHY AM I?

What is your purpose on earth? God has put all of us here on earth for a purpose. Generally God wants us to know Him and to fellowship with Him. He wants us to recover all that we have lost through Adam. God wants us to experience His grace in our lives. We are here because of what Jesus did at Calvary. We are here so that others can learn from our lives from the testimony of what

Jesus did for us and what He can also do for them. We are here to worship and adore the Lord. We are also here, to do battle with Satan.

The question is, what is your purpose as an individual? Have you found out from the Lord? A wasted life is a life without a purpose. Until your purpose for living is discovered, life may have no meaning. Your reason for being here on earth provides the key to your existence. These things must be clear in your spirit.

You cannot afford to live your life on experiment, or on trial and error. It is so short that you cannot experiment with it. You cannot afford to live on assumption. Pray again like this: " O Lord make my purpose for living plain before my face. I bind every spirit of aimlessness". You must know this fact, that the spirit of this age is the spirit of aimlessness. For everything you do in life, you must have a purpose for it; be it marriage, business, etc.

The reason there is so much confusion now is because people are outside God's purpose for their lives. They are busy pursuing their own little dreams. The carpenter is busy doing the driving job, and the painter is hell-bent on flying the aircraft. When this happens, a person's purpose is defeated, and things will not work the way they should.

## 5.     FROM WHERE AM I COMING?

Most people have not bothered to ask themselves, from where they came. Have you ever thought of that? Where is your origin? Although this is important many people nonetheless, do not think of their roots, that is, from where they came. It is certain that somebody who does not know from where he is coming would not know for where he is heading.

If for instance you do not know why you are a Christian, you will not know what you want in this life and thereafter. If your answer to the question: from where do you come is, I do not know, that is quite unsatisfactory. You must know your origin. The Bible makes it crystal clear that God created you and I. It has this to say,

> *"What is man, that thou art mindful of him? and the son of man, that thou visitest him? For thou hast made him a little lower than the angels, and hast crowned him with glory and honour. Thou madest him to have dominion over the works of thy hands; thou hast put all things under his feet."*
> Psalm 8:4-6

This tells us that man was created by God, and a time came when man lost all the glory of God and got into trouble. No matter how great a man is, his physical body is dust. The Lord told him, "Dust thou art and unto the dust thou shalt return". It is only the spirit of man that goes back to God. The next time you feel like boasting, remember, "Dust thou art and unto the dust thou shalt return". Let it be very clear in your spirit that whether a person is rich or poor, unto the dust shall he, or she return. We come from God, and that is to where we must compulsorily go back, unless the person is a rebel and does not want to go back to Him.

## 6.    WOULD I BE MADE WHOLE?

The last question is found in John 5:6. Jesus directed His question to a man who did not know Him (Jesus). The man was afflicted by the spirit of infirmity.

When Jesus saw him lie, and knew that he had been a long time in that case, he saith unto him, Wilt thou be made whole? Will you be made whole, too? If you say, Yes, I would like the Lord to make me whole, do you know He can do so this moment? But if you are happy and satisfied with the level you are now, you will never progress. When you know that God is calling you to climb higher, then you will dedicate yourself the more. You will be more committed, more prayerful, and you will increase your Bible reading time, your prayer time and your witnessing time. The Lord will help you in Jesus' name.

## 7. WHAT HAPPENS, WHEN I DIE?

The Bible answers the question. The Bible paints the picture of two places, and the contrast between them is frightening. The world we are in now is presently Satan's world. The kingdom of God will come and overcome this one. Jesus says clearly that when men die, they go to either of two places heaven, or hell fire. The Bible's graphic description of these two places, makes the contrast very clear. It is given to man to die only once, after that, judgement and it is better for a person not to be born at all, than to end up in hell fire. The Bible makes us to realise that when the rich man died, he found himself in hell fire, while Lazarus too died and found himself in the bosom of Abraham. Talk to the Lord in prayers like this: "Anything that will take me to hell fire, get out of my life now, in the name of Jesus"

## 8. WHEN THE SON OF MAN COMES, SHALL HE FIND FAITH IN ME?

This is found in Luke,

> *"And shall not God avenge his own elect, which cry day and night unto him, though he bear long with them? I tell you that he will avenge them speedily. Nevertheless when the Son of man cometh, shall he find faith on the earth?"*
> Luke 18:7-8

Let us make this question personal. When the Son of Man comes to us, shall he find faith in you and I? You can see that Jesus never answered that question. He just asked, and it is left for you and I to answer the question in our hearts. The angers of the last days caught up with many Christians. Supposing He comes today, since He may come at anytime, will he still find faith in your heart?

God is interested in our total life. He is interested in how well we are doing. Do you know the biblical truth that a thousand years in His sight is like a passing night? God has His own arithmetic. The question is, what do you weigh in His balance? How are you on His spiritual scale now? Are you a thermostat Christian, the type that the environment determines his temperature. While a thermostat Christian makes the environment to conform to him, he is not moved by what is happening around him.

What God needs first is our spirit man. The fire that has entered the spirit is sufficient to melt all problems away. How can fire enter into the spirit when the spirit is already blocked. What adjustment has God been asking you to make in your life? Has He been asking you to correct your thinking, dressing, speech, prayer life, or Bible reading?

Rise up today and do what the Lord wants you to do. Do not behave like a hypocrite, because the hopes of the hypocrites shall perish. If the trumpet shall utter an uncertain sound, the Bible says, who shall prepare for battle? What kind of fruit is your life producing? Are they positive that will attract people to the Lord, or are they fruits that will throw people down to the bottom of hell fire? You are going to open your mouth and pray aggressively the following prayer points, with your right hand on your chest.

## PRAYER POINTS

1. I refuse to let sin have dominion over me, in the name of Jesus.

2. I bind you spirit of anger, in the name of Jesus.

3. Lord, come into my heart in a different way, in the name of Jesus.

4. Every tree of spiritual failure, be uprooted, in the name of Jesus.

# CHAPTER 3

# CRY
## *your* WAY *to*
# GREATNESS

Whether are the other lessons, we can pick from the cry of arrest which blind Bartimaeus uttered?

## DO NOT WASTE TIME

Ask for the touch of the Lord while He is still around. That popular song says, "...While on others thou art calling, do not pass me by." Jesus never passed that way again. He was on His way to die. Bartimaeus had his last opportunity and made very good use of it. Many people hear the gospel not knowing that they could be hearing it for the last time. Perhaps if they had listened, they could have been saved.

## WIGGLESWORTH'S EXAMPLE

Brother Wigglesworth, who was an aggressive evangelist said that one day, God said to him, "Stand up, son and go into the market place. I have eleven souls to save through you today." He went to the market place and stayed there. As people were passing by, he kept asking the Lord, "Is it this one Lord?" If the Lord said, 'no', he would let the person go. But when the Lord said,

"Yes, that is the one," Wigglesworth in his known crude manner, would rush to the person and say, "Are you born again?" If his answer was, 'no', he would say to him, "You must get born again now." And right there in the market place, he would open the Bible, and begin to teach the person. Generally all the people he approached that way, gave their lives to Christ.

There was a day the Lord told him that eleven people would give their lives through him in the market place on that day. He got ten, and the eleventh person was not forthcoming before the market started closing and he too was getting impatient. He stood there until everybody went away from the market.

Suddenly somebody came along on a chariot, and the Lord said, "That is the man." Wigglesworth ran and jumped on the chariot. He said to the man, "It is because of you I have been waiting for so long, give your life to Jesus now," and the man said, "Yes, sir," and gave his life. Two days later, Wigglesworth saw in the newspaper that the man died the next day.

This is why spiritual opportunities are to be used to the fullest.

I do not believe that you are reading this book by chance, so the opportunity God has given to you to read this message must be used to the fullest. Jesus never passed that way again.

## LEARN TO CRY OUT

He understood the act of begging very well, and he applied it. If men will take the place of blind beggars before God and call for mercy, they will find it. The Bible says,

*"For whosoever shall call upon the name of the Lord shall be saved."* Romans 10:13

Sometimes all we need to do is to cry for God's mercy. His power is able to deliver. I like you to close your eyes again and pray like this: "Lord, have mercy upon me, in the name of Jesus."

## HAVE FAITH

The man had never seen Jesus before because he was blind, but, by faith he believed, and cried unto Him. It was first a cry, and later, he saw. The world's order of doing things is seeing before believing, but heaven's order is believing before seeing. When Martha said to Jesus, "If you had been here, my brother would not have died." Jesus answered her with a straight single sentence, "Thy brother shall live again." She said, "Yes I know he would rise again on the resurrection morning." And, Jesus said, "I am the resurrection. Said I not unto thee, that if thou wouldest believe, thou shouldest see the glory of God." Very simple, if you do not believe, the glory of God will be far away from you.

## DO NOT LET OTHERS KILL YOUR FAITH

Many people asked blind Bartimaeus to keep quiet, but he did not listen to them. The person who is saying, "A whole you," cannot lift one finger to help you out of your problem. There was one boy that used to come to Mountain of Fire and Miracles ministries, and his parents did not quite like it.

They tried to stop him, but could not, so they tried using charms. After putting some charms in their mouths, they woke the boy up at 12 midnight, and said, "Hear now, you will not go to that place again. Do you hear, as from today, the memory of that place will be removed from your brain, you will not go there again." While they went away rejoicing, the boy was laughing at their foolishness on his bed. The next day, he was the first to arrive here.

Millions of people are kept from heaven by the thought of what others will say. Sometimes when an altar call is made, some people will open their eyes, and first of all look around their surrounding to see whether there is anybody with his hand up before they raise theirs. When they cannot find any, they keep their hands down. This is how many people perish.

Some people come to crusades with their girlfriends and boyfriends, and when the word of God hits them where they are, they will not be able to come out because of their partners. Let it be clear to you that whether you do good or bad people will talk. Jesus said, "Woe unto you when they say that you are good." It means that you are one of them. But immediately you begin to live the kind of life God wants you to live, you will be criticised and attacked. If you are going to be listening to what people are saying or thinking about you before you serve the Lord, you will end up in trouble.

Millions of people are kept away from their breakthroughs, by listening to what others will say. God will hold you responsible if you allow your life to be directed by men. Bartimaeus refused to be influenced by those around him. He told them, "It is easy for you to be saying keep quiet, but I am the one that is blind." He screamed, and Jesus stopped.

## PERSEVERANCE

The Lord has a method of waiting for sometime, before He answers. Not because He does not know that there is problem, but He likes to test the reality of your desire. When you refuse to be discouraged, that is the mark of true faith. Some people fall under pressure.

A man had problems. One night, he felt so sad that he went to bed discouraged. As he slept he had a dream in which he found himself in a market place. At the market place he stumbled into a particular stall, with Mr. devil written on it, and the devil was there. The man said, "Mr devil, so you too are selling things in this market? The devil said, "Yes."

Then, he began to look at what he was selling, and saw items like hypertension, bad luck, cancer, all kinds of terrible things. He looked through, and said to the devil, "Hello, sir, what is the most expensive thing in your stall? He pointed at "discouragement," and told the man that when he wants to catch Christians he uses it. So when they get discouraged, their faith goes down, and they will not be able to pray and then fear will move in. And when that happens, worry will follow it, and, then, he, the devil, will move in. Discouragement is a powerful weapon of the enemy.

## VIOLENT FAITH

Another thing you can learn from this miracle cry of Bathimeaus is the principle of violent faith. Jesus said to him, thy faith has made you whole. Jesus healed him because he believed and asked. God honours faith. It is the appointed medium through which blessings come to us.

## HOLY HASTE

When Jesus told him to come, he moved like thunder, threw away his garment, so that it would not hinder him to come to Jesus. Remember in countries that are cold, beggars used to have lots of heavy clothing. So he had lots of things to discard. He pulled them off and started to move, and, then, his eyes got opened immediately, and he started seeing. You too can call upon Him before He passes by. And now, He is calling all men to repentance.

# CHAPTER 4

# STRATEGY
## *for* UNCOMMON
## GREATNESS

To attain uncommon greatness you need a strategy. This strategy must embrace efforts made towards paralysing the enemies of greatness. The fact that the enemy is wicked demands that we make use of uncommon methods. We must use the weapons of stones of fire. Stones of fire are the formidable weapons which the believer can use when the battle is toughest.

Tough battles require tough weapons. To survive on the field of battle, when the only means of survival is the use of an aggressive weapon, you must demonstrate uncommon wisdom. If you use a weak weapon to attack a formidable enemy, you will fail. Stones of fire are reserved for toughest moments on the field of battle. The weapon is required to kill stubborn Goliaths. You need prayers that are merciless and come in form of stones of fire.

When you haul such stones at the camp of the enemy, you will create quite a scene. There will be pandemonium, confusion and tragedy. Each stone of fire you throw will hit the target.

## HOLY STONES

Do you know that God himself had thrown stones at people before now?

> *"And it came to pass, as they fled from before Israel, and were in the going down to Beth-horon, that the Lord cast down great stones from heaven upon them unto Azekah, and they died: they were more which died with hailstones than they whom the children of Israel slew with the sword."* Joshua 10:11

God had to throw stones at people from heaven. Under what situation does God throw stones?

Please read this;

> *"And the Lord shall cause his glorious voice to be heard, and shall shew the lighting down of his arm, with the indignation of his anger,*

> *and with the flame of a devouring fire, with scattering, and tempest, and hailstones."* Isaiah 30:30

> *"Therefore thus saith the Lord God; I will even rend it with a stormy wind in my fury; and there shall be an overflowing shower in mine anger, and great hailstones in my fury to consume it."* Ezekiel 13:13

God throws stones when He is angry with the enemy. God's stones are special stones, they go back to heaven after they have done their work here, and stay there, waiting for the next stubborn enemy.

Do you want to successfully throw the stones of fire at your enemies? Then below are the conditions you need to fulfill to be able to do that.

1.   **You must give your life totally, to the Lord Jesus Christ.** Submit yourself to God as a living sacrifice.

2.  Put on the whole armour of God.

3.  Submit yourself completely to God, so that you can resist the devil.

> *"Neither give place to the devil."*
> Eph. 4:27

You must learn to do this always.

4.  Learn how to pray about everything.

5.  **Beware of gifts from unbelievers.** If you are still eating food prepared during non-biblical celebrations, then you need deliverance. Eating such food is like attending the party of the devil, and you have accepted the meal provided by him. The Bible says that all the meat that is sacrificed after the death of Christ is meal from the table of the devil.

6.  **Never pay ungodly visit to the territory of the enemy.** If you have commanded your enemies to receive stones of fire, and

you still go ahead to play in their territory, then you will partake in the stones of fire rain.

7.   **Learn to cast every burden on God, no matter what is happening.** Take your burdens to the Lord and leave them there. Then your stone throwing can be very effective.

What are the things that require the stones of fire? They are quite many, but the major ones will be listed for discussion.

1.   **Witches**

2.   **Wizards**

3.   **Satanic agents**

4.   **All the evil planners**

5.   **All the evil altars**

6.   **All the evil mouths**

7. All the satanic instruments and weapons.

8. All the evil observers sent to observe God's people.

9. All the eaters of flesh and drinkers of blood.

10. All the evil aid-de-camp that follow people around.

11. All the stubborn pursuers

12. ·All the masquerading problems

13. All evil marriage planners.

14. All the spirit husbands and Wives

15. Strange Children

16. Evil remote controllers

All these are qualified for the stones of fire. Let me assure you, that when you begin to throw the stones of fire, something definite must happen to your enemy; the kind of things that happened in the land of Egypt.

Now is the time to throw dangerous stones of fire at all your enemies. But for your stones to be effective you must be aggressive and do it with all your strength.

## PRAYER POINTS

When you call out the name of a particular thing, cry out loud, saying, "Receive the stones of fire, in the name of Jesus" twenty one times.

1.  All activities and powers of witchcraft spirit, present in my life now, (please lay your right hand on your head and left one on the chest) receive the stones of fire.
2.  All the plans and activities of wizards, and satanic agents, receive the stones of fire.
3.  Evil planners and evil altars, working against my life, at this moment, receive the stones of fire.

4. Satanic instruments and weapons fashioned against my life, receive the stones of fire.

5. All the eaters of flesh, and drinkers of blood, receive the stones of fire.

6. All stubborn pursuers, receive the stones of fire.

7. All problems manifesting, as masquerades, receive the stones of fire.

8. I will arise, and escape from the camp of the enemy, in the name of Jesus.

9. Thank God for answered prayers.

www.ingramcontent.com/pod-product-compliance
Lightning Source LLC
LaVergne TN
LVHW051203080426
835508LV00021B/2789